THE PLANET WE CALL HOME

Written by
Aimee Isaac

Illustrated by
Jaime Kim

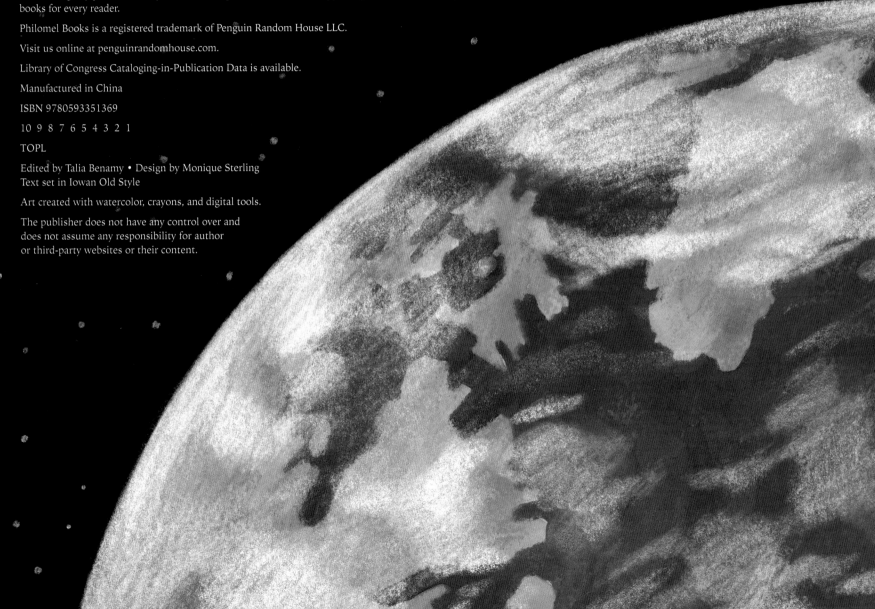

PHILOMEL
An imprint of Penguin Random House LLC, New York

First published in the United States of America by Philomel, an imprint of Penguin Random House LLC, 2023

Text copyright © 2023 by Aimee Issac • Illustrations copyright © 2023 by Jaime Kim

Visit us online at penguinrandomhouse.com.

Library of Congress Cataloging-in-Publication Data is available.

Manufactured in China

ISBN 9780593351369

10 9 8 7 6 5 4 3 2 1

TOPL

Edited by Talia Benamy • Design by Monique Sterling
Text set in Iowan Old Style

Art created with watercolor, crayons, and digital tools.

For my father, Ron Bowen, Environmental Steward —A. I.

For Lian —J. K.

This is our Earth,
the planet we call home.

These are the mountains
stretching from Earth,
the planet we call home.

This is the sun
that warms up the mountains
stretching from Earth,
the planet we call home.

This is the stream
that swells when the sun
warms up the mountains
stretching from Earth,
the planet we call home.

This is the farm
that nestles the stream
that swells when the sun
warms up the mountains
stretching from Earth,
the planet we call home.

This is the river, meandering by,
that flows past the farm
that nestles the stream
that swells when the sun
warms up the mountains
stretching from Earth,
the planet we call home.

This is the town, bustling and proud,
that greets the river, meandering by,
that flows past the farm
that nestles the stream
that swells when the sun
warms up the mountains
stretching from Earth,
the planet we call home.

This is the bay, bubbling with life,

that neighbors the town, bustling and proud,

that greets the river, meandering by,

that flows past the farm

that nestles the stream

that swells when the sun

warms up the mountains

stretching from Earth,

the planet we call home.

This is the ocean, vast as can be,

that joins with the bay, bubbling with life,

that neighbors the town, bustling and proud,

that greets the river, meandering by,

that flows past the farm

that nestles the stream

that swells when the sun

warms up the mountains

stretching from Earth,

the planet we call home.

This is the shore, swept by the breeze,

that meets the ocean, vast as can be,

that joins with the bay, bubbling with life,

that neighbors the town, bustling and proud,

that greets the river, meandering by,

that flows past the farm

that nestles the stream

that swells when the sun

warms up the mountains

stretching from Earth,

the planet we call home.

And these are the children, who cherish the Earth.
Who clean up the shore, swept by the breeze,
and study the ocean, vast as can be,
who wade in the bay, bubbling with life,
and speak in the town, bustling and proud,

who fish in the river, meandering by—
who visit the farm
        and splash in the stream,
                and use the sun,
as it warms up the mountains
        stretching from Earth . . .

SAVE THE EARTH

. . . which provides for us all,
wherever we are.

It's the planet we call **home**.

How Can We Prevent Pollution?

- Recycle! Find out more about the recycling program where you live, and follow its guidelines in school, at home, and everywhere you go.

- Reduce your use of plastic bags, straws, and balloons, and even try to stop using plastic altogether. Bring reusable bottles and bags to school, on shopping trips, and even when you travel!

- Save energy by turning off lights and unplugging electronics when they aren't in use.

- Reduce pollution by biking or walking instead of driving, and consider using cloth napkins to reduce waste.

- Conserve water by turning it off when you brush your teeth, and instead of pouring warm or stale water left in your water bottles down the drain, save it for your plants!

- Help clean up your neighborhoods and local natural areas (places like beaches, fields, and forests).

- Plant plants that are native to your region, which means they originally grew there naturally and weren't brought in from another faraway place.

- Learn how installing rain barrels and rain gardens in your community can help prevent precipitation from becoming dirty or polluted before it gets mixed in with other clean water.

- Eat food from local farms so that less energy is used to carry it from one place to another.

- Clean up after your pets so that their waste doesn't pollute your local waterways.

- Talk to farmers and local leaders about the ways in which trees and other plantings can help protect our waters.

- Teach others what you know! You have the power to make a difference and help save our planet for everyone who calls it home.

What will you do to teach others what you know?

Resources

Here are some websites that you can visit to find out more about our planet and what you can do to help protect it:

Ocean Facts, National Geographic Kids
natgeokids.com/uk/discover/geography/general-geography/ocean-facts

Pollution, National Geographic Kids
kids.nationalgeographic.com/explore/science/pollution

Rain Barrels, PBS Kids
pbskids.org/plumlanding/educators/context/131_build_a_rain_barrel.html

Rain Gardens, PBS
pbs.org/video/rain-garden-qoxhgh

Snowmelt Runoff and the Water Cycle, U.S. Geological Survey
water.usgs.gov/edu/watercyclesnowmelt.html

Streamflow and the Water Cycle, U.S. Geological Survey
water.usgs.gov/edu/watercyclestreamflow.html

Ten Tips to Reduce Your Plastic Use, National Geographic Kids
kids.nationalgeographic.com/explore/nature/kids-vs-plastic/10-tips
-to-reduce-your-plastic-use